A Voice for My Silent Lambs

By

Chandra R. Moyer

A Voice for My Silent Lambs
by Chandra R. Moyer

Printed in the United States of America

Library of Congress Control Number: 2002117035
ISBN 1-591603-41-2

Unless otherwise noted, Scripture quotations are taken from
the New American Standard Bible, The Open Bible,
Expanded Edition. Copyright © 1985 by Thomas Nelson,
Inc.

Scripture quotations noted NIV are taken from the Life
Application Bible, New International Version. Copyright ©
1988, 1989, 1991, Tyndale House Publishers.

Xulon Press
11350 Random Hills Road
Suite 800
Fairfax, VA 22030
(703) 279-6511
XulonPress.com

To order additional copies, call 1-866-909-BOOK (2665).

The accounts in this book are factual, however, to protect confidentiality, some of the names of people have been changed.

Illustrations by Dean Forbes

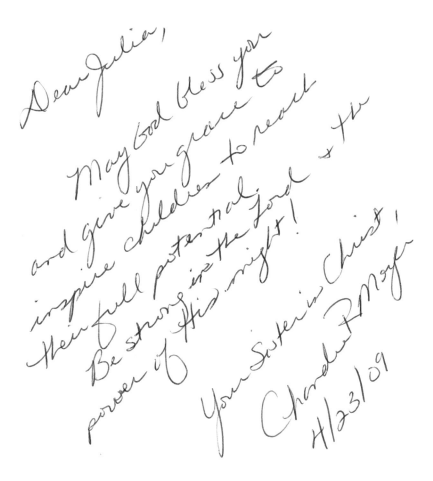

Dear Julia,

May God bless you and give you grace to inspire children to read their full potential + to Be strong in the Lord + to power if His might!

Your Sister in Christ,

Chandra P. Mayh

4/23/09

Contents

Acknowledgments

I want to first thank the Lord for giving me the opportunity to write this book and to speak on behalf of His children. What an honor and privilege it is to serve my Heavenly Father in this way. Although it has been a long labor, the birthing of this book has been worth all the pain and challenges to see this work completed.

My deepest gratitude to my husband, TP, who has supported my efforts to write this book and help turn this dream into a reality. Your patience and love has given me courage and strength to pursue God and all that He has for me.

To my three children, Aaron, Ashley and Micah who have seen me at my worse and still love me! You have taught me so much about unconditional love, more than you will ever know. You have brought incredible joy to my life and are precious to me. Thanks Ashley and Micah for sacrificing your time with me so that I could finish writing this book.

Heartfelt thanks, to Pastor Shirley Arnold, Janice Gach, Dreena Campana, Raycenia and Samuel Moyer who inspire me to continue to fulfill God's purpose and will for my life. To all my prayer partners I am forever grateful to you for seeing me through the years. Finally, to my dearest friend, sister, and intercessor, Linda Gaston who prayed and stood with me. Thank you for all your support and surrounding my family and me with prayer.

Preface

The purpose of this book is to bring public awareness to the critical condition of our nation's Child Protective Services and Foster Care System. An entire bureaucracy has sprung up to combat child abuse. Unfortunately, some of these efforts have backfired, seriously injuring the very children they were designed to protect. Very simply, the child protective system in most states is one that does not have the appropriate checks and balances required in the American judicial system. Where does one go to file a complaint against Department of Human Services (DHS)? Without that built-in safeguard, we have created a destructive bureaucratic agency that is often causing harm to the children they are entrusted to protect.

Like most Americans, I was unaware of the true condition of the child welfare agencies until my attempt to adopt a child in the state of Hawaii failed. In reality, we have too many children needlessly taken from their own homes in this country and placed in foster care. By telling our story, I hope to encourage other families who have been wounded by a system that has gone out of control. I pray that you will find comfort and healing in Jehovah Rapha, the God who heals.

He heals the brokenhearted and binds up their wounds. (Psalm 147:3)

CHAPTER 1

Call of the Innocent

In the spring of 1986, my husband TP received military orders that assigned us to Ft. Shafter, Hawaii, located on the island of Oahu. We had prayed for several months asking God to guide us to our next home and we knew in our hearts that this assignment came from our Commander-in-Chief, the Almighty God. Many soldiers ask to live in Hawaii, only to have their requests denied. Yet, TP was granted this prime assignment.

Although we were leaving our beautiful home in Stone Mountain, Georgia and our friends, we were excited about our new adventure and dreamed of spending many of our days on Hawaii's gorgeous beaches. TP and I had been married for eight years and were enjoying our lives with our two children (Aaron, age four, and Ashley, eight months). Since we never had a honeymoon, we anticipated our Hawaiian tour to be our romantic getaway. Unfortunately, our dream would shatter three years later.

Julie and Tommy were first brought to my attention

through a neighbor, Ann, in August of 1988. She and her husband Ron were in the process of adopting their second child when they noticed Julie and Tommy while visiting a foster home. Ann shared how TP and I kept coming to mind as she looked at the two children. She thought they would fit perfectly in our family because they resembled our birth children.

I felt a burden to pray for them and presented the prayer request to our neighborhood Bible study group. We prayed weekly that the Lord would help their birth mother to put her life together so that her children could return to her. A few weeks later, Ann came by my house to inform me that Julie and Tommy's birth mother's rights were terminated. The children were now wards of the state and eligible for adoption.

When our Bible study group gathered to pray that week, we asked God to bring a Christian family to adopt Julie and Tommy. One afternoon, Ann brought me a picture of the children. I felt my heart stir with compassion for these orphaned ones as she handed me the photo. Placing it on my kitchen counter, I was amazed at the striking resemblance to my own children. Every time I'd look at their picture throughout the day, I would pray for them and for their new family.

Surprisingly, by the end of September, I had a strong desire to adopt these children. At this point, I wasn't sure if the Lord had placed that desire in me or if it was an emotional response. TP showed no signs that he was interested in taking on two more children, while my compassion grew so intense that I began to pray that Jesus would remove this desire from me. But I also prayed that if this was His will, He would show TP and that we would be in agreement. Although we had two beautiful children, I didn't feel that our family was complete. During the birth of my second child, I was diagnosed with placenta previa. After going through eight hours of labor, I lost several units of blood and began to go into shock. An emergency c-section was performed and according to my doctor it was a miracle that Ashley lived. I was given transfusions and my recovery was slow. Based on the trauma surrounding Ashley's birth, the doctor recommended that I not have anymore children.

As a young girl, I dreamed that some day I'd grow up, marry, and adopt children. I truly believe God placed that desire in my heart. I can remember one night in college how I shared my desire with my future husband. He wasn't quite as enthusiastic about the adoption idea because he was content to have his own children.

On a Friday evening in October, the phone rang. I was in the shower when TP knocked on the door and yelled, "Ann's on the phone. She said that Julie and Tommy will be on the ten o'clock news tonight." Ann just happened to turn the TV channel during a commercial when she saw both children on a newsbreak.

The previous morning, I gave everything concerning the adoption to the Lord. I had cried out to God to remove the burden for these children because it was unbearable to me. TP showed no change and wasn't interested in knowing what God had put on my heart concerning them. He was already worried about how he was going to feed his two children and put them through college. On the other hand, I truly believed that if God were calling us to adopt these children, He would provide the finances.

Isn't that like God? He waits for us to completely surrender to Him and then He moves! Trembling, I dried myself. I felt God's presence and knew He was moving in a mighty way as I prayed in the spirit.

As we sat in front of our TV that night, we couldn't believe our eyes. Out of all the thousands of foster children in Hawaii, Julie and Tommy gazed at us through our TV screen. Stunned, we sat speechless, watching their foster parents hold them. Julie and Tommy's foster parents, along with many others, protested at the state capitol to demand that foster board payments be increased. When the report ended, I didn't say a word but arose and quietly walked to the bedroom. Before we went to sleep that night, TP took my hand and prayed for God's will concerning the adoption issue.

A few days later, TP asked me how I felt about Julie and Tommy. I shared the love I had for them and told him I believed God put it in my heart. Unaware that God had also been speaking to TP, he told me that everywhere he looked, he saw adoption. Even during a soccer game, he noticed a black boy calling to his parents who happened to be white. He knew the boy was adopted. TP said that he believed God was calling us to adopt Julie and Tommy, and that we needed to obey Him. It was the green light I needed to call the social worker who would administer the home study! Throwing my arms around his neck, I gave him a big hug, thanking him for his obedience to God!

Ann arranged our first meeting with the children. She had planned a celebration party for her newly adopted son and invited Julie and Tommy. The social worker agreed to this arrangement as long as the children weren't aware that we were interested in adopting them. Their foster parents were delighted that we were a military family because Julie and Tommy were biracial. They believed that the children would encounter difficult conditions because of their race if they remained in Hawaii.

Anticipating our first meeting, I anxiously peered out my kitchen window several times. Finally, I saw the children walking up the sidewalk with their foster parents. Although the children were young, they were accustomed to walking everywhere since their foster family didn't own a car.

Julie's two curly brown ponytails jiggled with each bouncy step. She seemed older than her years as she left her elderly foster parents trailing behind. Little Tommy tagged along behind them. I strained to see their little faces from the window as they walked past my house toward Ann's. Julie and Tommy were beautiful children with creamy mocha complexions. It was incredible how much they looked like my birth children. My heart melted, and an overwhelming desire rose up within me. I wanted to put my arms around them and shield them from the evils of this world. I know that God poured His compassion in my heart for those children that day.

We waited a few moments before walking to Ann's house to meet them. Although Julie was young, she showed that she was quite capable of taking care of herself. Refusing my help to remove the heavy plastic bag she carried, she struggled to carry it across the room and put it down.

Her foster parents introduced Julie and Tommy to us.

Looking up at me with her round chocolate eyes and her charming smile, Julie put her chubby little arms around my neck and hugged me. At the time, I didn't notice the emotional scars hidden behind her pretty face. This little girl was used to meeting strangers and felt comfortable around them. Strangers were all Julie had known during her three-and-a-half short years. She lived in and out of seven different foster homes, not including shelters.

Ann suggested that we walk to the neighborhood playground so that the children could play, and we agreed. In recalling that day, the incident on the jungle gym returns vividly to my mind. We were having a wonderful time watching the children play together. Tommy, age two-and-a-half, went off to himself but my oldest son, Aaron, kept bringing him back with the group. We thought it was cute how Tommy covered his face when we'd talk to him because he was so shy. Julie had climbed quite high on the bars of the jungle gym and her whine indicated that she couldn't get down. I felt that she was too heavy for me to lift, so I called TP over for help. When he stretched out his arms to reach her, she pulled away and hissed at him like a cat. I felt uneasy about her reaction, but I excused it as I thought to myself, she just isn't used to being around men.

Many times I doubted my ability to mother four children. While driving my son to school one morning, I questioned the Lord. "Why are You calling us to adopt these children? I don't know if I can rear four children. It's not easy raising my two kids. Besides, I struggle with patience and need a nap to get through the day." I heard the Lord reply, "These children need you very much and you need them. My grace is sufficient for you, for power is perfected in weakness. I am molding you into the person I want you to be. You need these children to help you to become that person." As I listened to His voice, I had a vision. I saw his beautiful, loving hands holding me, and shaping me into His image. Tears of joy trickled from my eyes as I experienced His tender love.

I returned home, and I picked up my Bible reading from the previous day. Jeremiah 18:6 spoke to me in such a profound way. I heard the Spirit say to me, *"Can I not, Chandra, deal with you as the potter does?" declares the Lord. "Behold, like the clay in the potter's hand, so you are in my hand, Chandra."*

This passage of scripture confirmed the vision and what He had spoken to me earlier that day in the car. I was in awe of God and that He would speak so tenderly. As the potter shapes and molds the clay in His hands, the Lord would mold and fashion me into His image. I wept as I surrendered all my fears and inadequacies to Him.

We prayed continuously as we proceeded through the adoption home study. Mrs. Smith, the social worker who handled our home study, was very pleasant and helpful. In fact, she encouraged us to seek help from a psychologist in the future concerning the children. Everything proceeded quickly and with ease. Now that the home study was completed, we were officially approved as prospective adoptive parents. The adoption process would take anywhere from six months to a year to finalize.

We had a couple of visits with the children to ensure that the transition from one home to the other would go as smooth as possible. By now their foster parents and social worker had told the children that we were their new family. On one visit in particular, I noticed the strain of adjusting to another family on Julie. It was our first outing alone with the children. We took them to the beach and then to McDonald's for ice cream. On the drive back to their foster home, I noticed Julie looked exhausted and detached. As we dropped them off and waved goodbye, I heard Julie's foster mother say, "You better say goodbye to your new family or they might not want you." My heart broke as I watched Julie turn around and frantically wave goodbye as we pulled out of the driveway.

The initial meeting with Mrs. Won, the children's social worker, was unsettling. She was in her mid-forties with a formal, aloof demeanor that lacked any sign of warmth. I had prepared a list of questions concerning Julie's and Tommy's past. How many homes had the children lived in? How did the birth mother feel about losing her children? Were they physically or sexually abused? Mrs. Won was clearly more interested in discussing her daughter's upcoming visit to the Soviet Union than offering us information about the children's past. The only answers we received were that the children were removed from their birth mother due to neglect. According to Mrs. Won, the birth mother showed very little emotion at the hearing and wasn't upset that her children were to be placed for adoption. The information about their background was sketchy. She told us that both parents were homeless and lived in a car for a short time. "There was no evidence of sexual or physical abuse, only neglect. The birth mother doesn't care about her children. I want to make it clear to you that you have no rights as prospective adoptive parents. Everything you do with the children must meet with my approval." Among the many things that were made clear to us that day was that Mrs. Won shared none of our enthusiasm about the children's arrival.

CHAPTER 2

Silent Lambs

Finally, the special day arrived. Julie and Tommy were coming home! My birth son Aaron, age seven, and daughter Ashley, age three, were excited about their new brother and sister. They had helped me prepare Julie and Tommy's bedrooms. On December 31, 1988, we picked the children up at their foster home. Julie showed no regret in leaving her foster parents. The children had been prepared and were told that their new parents would take care of them. The social worker and foster parents told them that they would never have to change families again. Julie ran right up to me, hugged me, and jumped into the car. I would later learn that her behavior indicated her inability to bond.

I can still remember the feeling of love that swept through me when we brought Julie and Tommy into our home that sunny December day. Our home truly felt like Christmas. That night we tucked the children into bed and we said their prayers with them, thanking Jesus for bringing them into our lives.

Two days later, we returned to their foster home to pick up the rest of their toys. When we pulled up in the driveway, Julie and Tommy jumped out of the car and grabbed their bikes. They dragged them back to our car and sat down. The only thing Julie said to her foster mother was, "I don't live here anymore. I live with Aunti Chandra now, and I've got new shoes."

During the first week, it felt like a long-awaited vacation. Everyone was happy and excited. Julie tried so hard to please us and was continually sitting on my lap. However, her actions were mechanical, lacking emotion. Initially, I thought Julie was adjusting very quickly. I would later learn from a psychologist that Julie's eagerness to leave her foster parents for two strangers was a sign of an "unattached" child. Children with attachment disorders are unable to bond with their parents and incapable of forming intimate relationships. They often feel intense inner rage and hatred.

Tommy, on the other hand, was quite distant, which is a normal response toward strangers. He didn't allow anyone close to him. When we'd pick him up, he would say, "I'm too big; put me down." I realized that he had been told he was too big to carry and wasn't used to anyone holding or cuddling him. But it didn't take long for him to get used to the idea that we loved to hold him. He blossomed into an affectionate little boy.

Within a few weeks, the atmosphere in our home began to change. The trauma that Julie had experienced manifested itself in different ways. She had terrible nightmares. Julie would wake up crying hysterically, "They are fighting and he's going to get me!" As I held her close, I could feel her little heart pounding. "What had this child seen to make her so frightened?" I wondered.

Another time as we prepared to go to the grocery store, Julie deliberately hit herself so hard that she got a black eye. I noticed that she avoided my eyes when I talked with her. To get her attention, I'd place my hand under her chin and turn her face toward mine to make eye contact. But often she would respond with a blank stare, a glazed look. I felt so helpless in dealing with Julie's frequent tantrums that seemed to escalate beyond her control. Nothing I said or did would console her.

When I shared with the social worker my concerns about Julie, she assured me that all Julie needed was a good home and a lot of love. Her behavior was part of the adjustment phase and I just needed to lower my expectations. I felt that my parenting skills were lacking in this area and I needed some professional guidance to reach Julie. When I suggested that I take Julie to a child psychologist, I was shocked at Mrs. Won's response: "I forbid you to take her to a psychologist! I don't believe Julie needs that type of help. I think you just need to continue to love her and things will get better." On the contrary, things didn't get better—they only got worse.

A month after the children's arrival, their guardian ad litem came to visit. She was responsible for the well being of the children and represented them in court. In other words, she spoke on their behalf. The guardian, who was also an attorney, was thrilled that they were in our home. "You have no idea where these children came from. I'm so happy they are in a beautiful and loving home." The information she gave us painted a different story and her facts concerning Julie's past contradicted Mrs. Won's. The guardian cautioned me about the birth mother because she was very upset about losing them. She feared that the birth mother would react violently if she saw me with her children. Since the island of Oahu was small, she warned me to be careful where I took them.

The most disturbing information was the environment of Julie's first foster home where she had lived for a year. The guardian had to abruptly remove Julie from this home without notice because of prostitution and drug activity. She had physically pried Julie away from her foster mother as she screamed and cried. The guardian admitted how disturbed she had been about Julie's removal and had lain awake nights wondering what effect this had on her. She believed that Julie's removal from her first foster home had caused her severe trauma.

My concern was of the effect and trauma she may have suffered while living there. If not in her first home, what about the other places she lived? My suspicion was confirmed that Julie had been sexually abused in one of her previous homes. That also explained her negative reaction toward TP when she first met him.

I'll never forget the day when I called, "Julie, come here." She turned around and looked at me and said, "I'm not Julie. I'm Sissy." Her expression told me that she wasn't pretending to be Sissy—she was Sissy.

"Where is Julie?" I asked.

"She's not here. She went somewhere."

Chills went down my back as I looked into her eyes and

saw another personality. Frightened, I called my husband at work and told him that Julie was no longer responding to her name.

Julie had a terrible persistent cough when she came to us. I had taken her to the doctor several times, and she was treated with variety of antibiotics without success. I kept pressing the social worker for the children's medical history. Finally, she gave in. It was then that we learned that Julie was a premature baby and had been on a respirator that caused some scarring to her lungs. With this information, the doctor was able to provide the correct medication for her and the cough subsided.

Tommy was an adorable, stout little fellow who loved walking through the house singing songs about Jesus. Although he had a few problems, we felt that he was adjusting to our family. One day after Tommy awoke from his nap, I scooped him up into my arms. He laid his head on my shoulder and wrapped his chubby arms around my neck. My heart melted as tears stung my eyes. This was the first time Tommy had reached out to anyone to be loved. He wouldn't let go of me and I held him close that entire afternoon.

Tommy loved to play house and dress up with the girls. Initially he showed very little interest in Aaron. Noticing his attachment to dress up in girl clothes, one morning I asked him if he was a girl or a boy. Tommy answered with a big grin, "I'm a goil!" It dawned on me that he had no idea he was a boy. I explained to him that he was a boy like Aaron and Daddy. As soon as TP and Aaron came home that day, they all had a powwow in the bathroom! From then on, Tommy would run around and yell, "I'm a boy, I'm a boy!"

He became Aaron's little shadow and the mascot of Aaron's soccer team.

Many times, I found myself on my knees praying to the Lord for strength and wisdom on how to rear four children. Amazingly, my energy level increased tremendously. TP couldn't believe the amount of energy I had, and we both knew God had poured out His grace on me because I was no longer taking naps. I've learned through the years that whatever assignment God gives us, He always equips us with the resources to accomplish the task.

We had two lovely additions to our family who needed more than just the love it took to "make them better." We as their parents sincerely wanted to understand and meet all their needs, but the battle seemed overwhelming as we faced these issues alone without the support of the state agency.

Friends of ours who had adopted a five-year-old child from foster care years ago suggested that we seek help immediately for both children. They wished that someone had given them similar advice when their daughter was young. This mother was living a nightmare in her own home. Her sixteen-year-old daughter suffered from destructive behavior such as self-mutilation, excessive lying, and lack of conscience (unconcerned about hurting others or destroying things). Now the entire family was suffering because of their daughter's destructive behavior. No one outside the family would ever suspect that this was happening in their home because their daughter appeared so normal and charming to members outside the family.

One of the major problems we found working with the state agency was that they didn't see the need to provide full disclosure on the children, including medical histories. We felt that vital information had been withheld from us, which made it difficult to understand Julie's behavior and effectively help her.

In addition to this, I began to feel paranoid when I took the children on excursions, afraid I'd run into their birth mother and she'd react violently toward me. According to the guardian ad litem, the birth mother showed up at social services, threatened the social worker, and demanded that her children be returned. Despite the bizarre circumstances I found myself in, I knew God had brought these children into our lives and I was determined to get help for Julie.

We met with Mrs. Won again and insisted that she give us permission to take Julie to a child psychologist. Defiantly, she said, "You have to decide whether or not you want to keep these children. There are many other families who would love to have them." A sick feeling stirred in the pit of my stomach. I thought, "She's emotionally blackmailing us. Indirectly she is threatening to remove the children if we don't obey her rules."

Startled by her response, my husband and I explained to her how we loved and wanted the children. The real issue was that the children needed help! We expressed how upset we were that she didn't give us all the facts concerning the children's past. How could we effectively help the children when pertinent information was withheld from us? We told her how only a week earlier, we had watched Julie draw pictures of both male and female genitals, explaining how they come together. We shared our shock and our fears with her and, now knowing the truth concerning the children's past, we were more convinced that Julie needed professional counseling.

After refusing my request to take Julie to a private psychologist, Mrs. Won reluctantly scheduled a meeting with Dr. Chung, the Department of Human Services psychologist. Later that week we met with Dr. Chung. By this time, the stress level in our home had increased significantly. Not only was I struggling with fears of my own inadequacies in raising a child with such major emotional issues, but I also felt anger toward this agency's lack of support in helping these children. We expressed our frustrations about the resistance we felt from the social worker in providing help for Julie. Dr. Chung evaluated Julie for fifteen minutes and refused to discuss his diagnosis with us until he had first spoken with the social worker. When we walked out of his office, I told TP that his evaluation was a joke and we probably wouldn't hear from him. Sure enough, we received a call from Mrs. Won, informing us that the psychologist's evaluation showed that there was nothing wrong with Julie and that she had not been traumatized by the system. It was amazing to us that Dr. Chung could make such a diagnosis in one short visit. What became very clear to us was that the agency was more concerned with covering up their mistakes than helping these innocent children.

Since I felt that we were hitting a brick wall in communicating our concerns for the welfare of these precious children to Mrs. Won, I decided to call her supervisor on February 23, 1989. When her supervisor refused to meet with us, I called the unit administrator who was unavailable. I left a message with her secretary requesting that she return my call. Every day I became more frustrated and angry with Mrs. Won. Her lack of compassion for the children and her obvious lack of integrity were appalling to us. One morning, Mrs. Smith, who administered the home study, called to apologize for all the misinformation we received from the department and wanted to help. "Why don't you enroll in the foster to adopt program, since you weren't told the truth about the children's past. This way it would be easier to get Julie the necessary help she needs. I'll discuss this with Mrs. Won," she said.

"You mean that the system will provide assistance if I'm a foster parent, but denies access to resources if I'm an adoptive parent? That's just ludicrous. But if that's the only way we can get help for Julie, I'm willing to go this route temporarily. I want to make it clear we still want to adopt these children. However, I don't want to wait a year until the adoption process is finalized before taking Julie to counseling," I explained.

Later that day, Mrs. Smith called back and said, "I can't believe that Mrs. Won was totally against my recommendation. She feels that this shows lack of commitment on your part. I disagreed with her and explained that we need to help you any way we can concerning the circumstances."

Around this same time, their foster mother called to say she had Tommy's medical card. When I questioned her about Julie's behavior, her story changed. "Julie has all kinds of problems, and you'll need all the help you can get for the next eighteen years in raising her. She is a difficult child and often has screaming fits."

"Why didn't you tell me this information about Julie

earlier?" I asked. "You told me how bright and smart she was."

"The social worker told me that I couldn't tell you anything about her behavior, so I didn't. But she is really slow on day-to-day activities, and I had all kinds of problems with her," she said.

I hung up the phone in disbelief. I felt overwhelmed about how to cope with Julie's behavior. Much of my energy and time were directed toward Julie's needs and fighting the system to get her help. The resistance from Mrs. Won was like having my hands tied behind my back. At every turn, I was discouraged from seeking help by Mrs. Won. I spoke again to their guardian about the difficulty we had with Mrs. Won. She agreed with me that both Julie and Tommy should be in therapy. She said she could help in that area. According to her, the birth mother also used cocaine and that could be part of Julie's problem.

CHAPTER 3

Secret Meeting

By the end of February, the tension in our home was very high, and TP was concerned about my well being. The amount of energy and time it was taking to raise Julie and deal with Mrs. Won was taking its toll on our other children and me. TP and I agreed that the quality of our lives was deteriorating rapidly and we didn't have the resources or strength to fight this powerful system. We called Mrs. Won and told her that we decided to accept Mrs. Smith's suggestion to transfer into the foster to adopt program based on all the misinformation, lack of support, and adverse conditions we were dealing with in the system.

"You don't sound very committed, and there are many other families out there waiting to adopt these children," she said. "I have to speak with my supervisor, and I don't know when I can see her." This conversation upset TP so much that it was very difficult for him to return to work. Mrs. Won's lack of sensitivity toward the children and to us became more frustrating every day. We requested that she have her supervisor call us. Her immediate supervisor never returned any of our calls, so we then called the unit administrator.

About a week after our disturbing conversation with Mrs. Won, I received an upsetting call from the guardian on March 1. "Chandra, please pray. Mrs. Won has arranged a secret meeting, and her intention is to remove the children permanently from your home. You're the only hope for these children." I told her about Mrs. Won's threats about how there were so many families wanting to adopt them.

"There are no other families wanting biracial siblings. If you don't adopt them, the chance of them being adopted is very slim."

"Why can't you speak on behalf of the children?" I asked. "As their guardian, surely you can defend these children!"

"It's not worth fighting the social workers because they have so much power. It won't do any good to fight them. I don't believe Mrs. Won will change her mind because she feels she has to be in control," she said.

"I'm not bonding with Julie, and I don't like the fact that I'm having negative feelings toward her due to my frustrations with her behavior and the system. I'm too tired to fight anymore. We need help, and if the system is not willing to help us, than maybe it's best to find another family for Julie where there are no other children so she can receive the special attention that she needs. As much as we love Tommy, and even though he has bonded with us, I understand the agency wants to keep them together. I'm very angry and saddened that we haven't been given a chance to make this adoption situation work!

I hung up the phone in tears. I felt so guilty that I had failed as a mother to Julie and Tommy. I also felt embarrassed, because I had told my neighbors that God had led us to adopt these children. Now it appeared that we would lose them. Not only did I feel like I'd failed the children, but I had also failed God.

The next day, I received a call from Mrs. Taka, the Unit Administrator. I explained to her that it was too late—a decision was made the previous day to make us foster parents and to find another family for the children. Supposedly, Mrs. Won based her decision on the fact that this was not a good match between prospective adoptive parents and children. I emphasized to her that this was not our desire. Mrs. Taka apologized for taking so long (nine days) to return my call, but she had been extremely busy and called the first chance she got. Mrs. Taka wanted to know our story.

After I told her everything she asked, "Is Julie in therapy?"

"No she's not," I replied. "Mrs. Won has refused to allow me to take her to a psychologist."

"She should be in play therapy now. And I can't believe that Mrs. Won made those threats to you because she recently came to us highly recommended. You've had the children for only two months, and it's too early to make a decision to move the children. Your feelings toward Julie are normal, and bonding with her will take some time, especially after what she's been through," she said. "I'm concerned about Tommy. How is he doing?"

"Tommy is getting along very well," I answered. "He is part of the family and is already bonding with us. The children are now calling us Mommy and Daddy. Their social worker told them they would never switch families again. I don't know what this move will do to Julie, and the guardian expressed this same concern."

"This move will also hurt Tommy, now that he has bonded with you."

Mrs. Taka asked if the children were black. When I told her they were, she informed me that we should have received financial assistance from the beginning. They are considered special needs children because, as biracial children, they are difficult to place for adoption. After I told her about the misinformation we received, she agreed that these were major issues and that we should have been given these facts from the beginning. Mrs. Taka believed the board acted too hastily in their decision to remove the children, and she agreed to investigate this situation. She would get back to me.

That same day, I called a child psychologist who was referred to me by a foster parent. When I explained Julie's behavior to her, she agreed that Julie needed to be in therapy now. According to the psychologist, as Julie's prospective adoptive parent, I had the right to take her for counseling without the social worker's permission.

A few days later, I took Tommy to the pediatrician for a checkup and told him everything that happened with social services. His response was that Dr. Chung was in a difficult position because he was on the DHS team and on their payroll. In other words, Dr. Chung's evaluation of Julie would reflect what the social worker wanted.

Finally, I got the courage to take Julie to the psychologist.

At this point, I felt we had nothing to lose since Mrs. Won had decided to take the children from us. The psychologist spent an hour with Julie. She said Julie had memory blocks and barriers. However, she felt that she could work with Julie and me to help us bond. I was encouraged by this good news. The psychologist was concerned about my desire to save Julie. "I want you to think about why you're willing to fight the entire system to protect Julie. It seems as though you have met Julie in the past. Could it be that she reminds you of yourself?" Initially, I thought her statement was very strange, but I would learn a few years later that Julie stirred something deep within me. She touched a part of me that I'd forgotten.

The next morning while I was brushing Julie's hair, the phone rang.

"This is Mrs. Won. I've found another family for the children, and I will pick them up next Monday." Click. She hung up.

Shaken, I placed the phone on the hook. My stomach churned as I felt panic rise from the pit of my stomach. "What's happening? Why does Mrs. Won want to move the children so quickly? Why the secrecy surrounding the children's new family? Why couldn't we meet the new parents to help smooth the transition for the children?" Those were the thoughts racing through my mind as I finished brushing Julie's hair.

I didn't want the children to see how angry and upset I was, so I tried to keep my voice calm as I finished dressing Julie and the other children. I drove Julie to preschool and dropped the other two children at a friend's house to play.

When I returned home, I called TP at work to tell him the bad news. He was angry, so he came home and called Mrs. Won to ask her why we weren't given at least two weeks' notice. Seven days ago they didn't have a family, and suddenly they had one? He suggested that the children have several visits in their new home to make this transition as smooth as possible. Mrs. Won was adamant about her decision.

TP is normally very even-tempered, but I could see he was about to explode over the phone with Mrs. Won. TP had received a phone call the previous night from his mother informing him that his stepfather was to undergo open-heart surgery. He told Mrs. Won that he didn't need all this added frustration with the agency. Since she had made it clear to us that we had no rights as prospective adoptive parents, he suggested that she pick up the children on Friday rather than having us deal with the agency over the weekend.

I felt helpless as I sobbed, "Lord, why is this happening to us? We've only done what You called us to do, and now our family is being torn apart!" There was no answer—only silence. I truly felt God had abandoned me.

Later that day, a thought came to mind that I should contact the media with our story. Recently, several news stations had covered stories about the problems that plagued the Department of Human Services. I now know it was the Holy Spirit who prompted me to make that call. I spoke with a news reporter from a local TV station, and he was interested in our story. He asked that I keep him informed. A few months earlier, I had filed newspaper articles that addressed the many problems in Hawaii's foster care. I pulled out those clippings and contacted the journalist who wrote those articles. She was out of town, so I left a message on her answering machine.

I felt our only hope now was to appeal to the Director of Human Services. I explained to her secretary that I was filing a formal complaint against the department and I wanted to make an appointment with the director. Initially, my request was denied until I informed her secretary that I'd already spoken to the media. I was granted a hearing with the director that afternoon.

TP and I arrived at the director's office with Julie and Tommy at 2:30 p.m. The secretary watched them as we met with the director and the Oahu branch administrator, Ms. Loy. The moment I walked into the director's office, I felt an evil presence. Most of the conversation was one sided as we shared our story with her. When TP asked her for the department's side of the story, she told us that she would investigate our complaint and that the children would remain with us until then. As we walked out of the building, I told TP I had felt an evil and oppressive presence that came from the director.

CHAPTER 4

Systems of Injustice

The very next morning, the phone rang at the same time that someone knocked on my front door. It was a classic setup. I answered the phone to hear Ms. Loy, the branch administrator, explain that they had investigated our complaint and decided to proceed with Mrs. Won's recommendation.

"You can't take the children. We haven't talked with them about moving yet!" I exclaimed. As I talked on the phone, Mrs. Won and another woman entered my home and began to ask Tommy where Julie was. The smirk on Mrs. Won's face made me want to slap her! It was only God's grace that prevented me from physically attacking her.

I asked the administrator why Mrs. Won was at my door, because we were told the day before that everything was on hold until the investigation was completed. There was no way they could effectively investigate our complaint overnight. "No one is taking the children anywhere, and I suggest you talk with Mrs. Won and tell her to leave my home now!" I spat.

I handed Mrs. Won the phone and ushered Tommy and Ashley into another room. After Mrs. Won spoke briefly with the administrator, she handed me the phone. I told Ms. Loy I would call her back and hung up the phone.

Glaring at Mrs. Won, I said in a low tone, "There must be some misunderstanding, and I suggest you leave my home right now." They left without a word. I knew that they had expected a theatrical scene, and it would have given them ammunition to possibly use against me at a later date.

I trembled as I made the call to TP. I could hardly tell him what happened without sounding hysterical. He came home immediately. When TP walked through the door, I threw myself into his arms. Pounding his chest with my fist in outrage, I sobbed, "They are taking our babies, and there's nothing we can do to stop them! I've failed as a mother to Julie and Tommy." An excruciating pain seared my heart. Nauseated, I ran to the bathroom, gasping for breath. The evil wrapping its ugly web around me was suffocating.

"Chandra," pleaded TP, "There's nothing else we can do. We have no rights as their prospective adoptive parents, and I have no more strength to continue to fight the system. Our family is falling apart, and I'm worried about how this is affecting you emotionally. I think that it's best for them to come and pick up the children this afternoon."

He went into the other room to call the administrator. TP requested that they send a social worker other than Mrs. Won. I sat on the couch thinking, "This is a nightmare and I'll wake up at any moment." But it wasn't a dream—it was harsh reality. I'll never forget that day or understand it. We sent our daughter Ashley to a neighbor's house to play. We didn't want her to see the children being taken away by strangers.

I felt as though my body was shutting down emotionally, and all I could do was sit at the piano and play. It was difficult for me to see the notes on the page through all the tears. I felt a presence at my elbow and looked down. Tommy looked up at me with his round, dark eyes, and questioned, "Why is Daddy putting all my things in bags?"

I stopped playing and tenderly gazed at his chubby face. I swallowed the lump rising in my throat and explained, "You and Julie will move to another house this afternoon."

Already I felt myself emotionally pulling away from Tommy. My heart broke because I wanted to hold him in my arms, yet I couldn't. I didn't want to fall apart in front of him and I felt I needed to be strong for him.

Moments later, I picked up Julie from preschool and explained to her that we were headed to Aaron's school so she could say goodbye to him. She sat silently as I told her that she was moving to another home. How could I explain to the children what was happening when I couldn't grasp it myself? Nothing made sense, and it seemed so irrational. Although I lived in America, I felt I was living in a communist country where the government has unlimited power.

I'll always remember the perplexed expression on Aaron's face when I called him off the playground to say goodbye to Julie and Tommy. Later I'd realize that leaving Aaron at the playground to deal with his emotions alone was not a wise decision. At the time, we thought we were protecting Aaron by leaving him at school so he wouldn't see his brother and sister taken away in a strange white car.

During his senior year in high school, Aaron wrote in a school paper what happened on that tragic day:

> Little did I know that March 9, 1989, would be the saddest day of my life. I was running around playing with my friends during third-grade recess, when my mom came onto the playground and walked me over to the school parking lot. There she stood, with my little brother Tommy and my little sister Julie. In those few moments in the school parking lot, I found out that it would be the last time I would see little Tommy and Julie.
>
> My mom told me to say goodbye, so I did with a hug and kiss, and just like that, they were gone. Deeply hurt, I somberly walked back to the playground and finished my day at school. Though they were with us basically a short period of time, it seemed a lot longer to me, and I became strongly attached to them. It wasn't until five years after the tragedy when I released all my anger and other emotions that had been hidden inside.

TP and I gathered the last of their toys and bikes and tried to be optimistic for the children's sake. Julie asked me, "Mommy, can you fix my hair in two ponytails for school tomorrow?"

"Julie, tell the new lady you'll live with how you like to wear your hair," I choked.

On March 9, 1989, TP and I gathered the last of the children's belongings and sat down to hold them for one last time. We shared how much we loved them and that Jesus would take care of them in their new home. We laid hands on them and prayed for God's protection. Since the children like to sing, TP led us in singing "Jesus Loves Me." Tommy had such a big voice for a two-year-old. I can still hear his voice singing, "Yes, Jesus loves me, the Bible tells me so."

TP advised me to leave the house before they came to pick up the children. I knew that he was trying to spare me from further pain, but I knew I needed to stay home. I was so fragile emotionally and I didn't want to go anywhere for fear I would fall apart in public. So we decided that I should remain upstairs.

Moments later, the white car pulled up to our curb and I ran upstairs into Aaron's room that faced the street. As much as it hurt, I wanted to see my children one last time. I stood at the window and watched as the social worker loaded the car and then rounded up the children. TP walked them to the car and helped buckle their seatbelts. I saw Julie reach over and hug TP. It was the first time that she really hugged him. Tommy's expression was a solemn one as he hugged his Dad goodbye.

In anguish I cried out, "Lord, they are taking our children away and destroying them!" I heard Jesus reply, "Yes, they're hurting My children, but how many more children are being destroyed?" Immediately, I saw not only my two children, but also a sea of children caught up in this destructive system. I wept bitterly for all God's children lost in this system, knowing they will never know the true meaning of love or what it means to trust.

Late that afternoon, three officials called from the

Department of Human Services. "I'm returning your call from the other day," Mrs. Taka said, acting as if she didn't know what was happening.

"Haven't you heard that they took the children this afternoon?" I asked.

"Yes, I did, and I'm sorry. I need to know when the children were placed in your home. My records show January 12, 1989," she said.

"Your records are inaccurate, because they came in our home on December 31, 1988. Mrs. Won didn't come to our house with the adoption agreement until January twelfth, and therefore dated the document as such."

"I'd like to pay you for taking care of the children as foster parents and make it retroactive to December thirty-first."

"I don't want your filthy money!" I spat. "What I want is an explanation. Why didn't you call me back after we talked on March second, when you said that you were going to conduct an investigation and get back with me? Instead of hearing from you, I got a call from Mrs. Won saying that she found another home for the children."

"The decision to remove the children was made based on Dr. Chung's evaluation that Julie was normal. I want to thank you for all the hard work you've done. All this information will be helpful in placing Julie and Tommy in their new—"

"Help me to understand why you removed Julie and Tommy in such a cruel way."

"Sorry, we're not able to discuss the reasons with you. You'll need to talk with Mrs. Smith about it."

"We're concerned about the next family. What happens when they begin to ask questions? Are you going to uproot the children again and say it was a mismatch? How can this be in the best interest of the children?" I pleaded. "Why has everything been so secretive? We believe the agency is covering up their mistakes at the expense of children's lives. All the threats that Mrs. Won made against us have come true!"

Never once did Mrs. Taka address the issue, and not one of the officials gave us an explanation that day. It's very difficult for me to remember the details of the rest of that afternoon; it seems like a blur. However, that night is stamped firmly in my mind. When I tucked Aaron into bed, he looked across the hall into Tommy's room and cried, "Mom, I miss Tommy." I held Aaron close in my arms and whispered, "I miss him, too."

CHAPTER 5

Courage to Stand

The next morning, I arose early to write to numerous government officials concerning the injustices in the Department of Human Services. I engulfed myself in this endeavor so that I would not feel the pain. TP pleaded with me to lay it aside to be with him and our children because they needed me. It was difficult to let the writing go and embrace my children. Hesitantly, I laid down my papers and held Aaron and Ashley close to my heart. By doing so, I was embracing the pain of knowing I had two missing.

I know it was God's grace that carried me through the next few weeks. One day I found myself yelling at Aaron and Ashley. I watched, as if in slow motion, Aaron walking in one direction and Ashley in the opposite. A thought flashed across my mind: "Satan not only wants to destroy Julie and Tommy's lives but your entire family with this calamity." I said aloud, "Satan, I bind you in Jesus' name. You have no claim on our family. The blood of Jesus washes us, and we are His children. We will be a closer family because of this crisis and closer to Jesus!" I gathered my children and held them as we cried. I praise God that He took the scales off my eyes and allowed me to see the spiritual warfare we faced, but it was only the beginning.

A week after the children's removal, my neighbor Ann stopped by for a short visit to check on me. It amazed me how God used her to provide valuable information. She gave me her issue of the *Ladies' Home Journal* and suggested that I read the article, "We're Afraid of Our Son." It addressed the issue of disclosing medical and abuse history to adoptive parents. In hopes that others would not have to share their suffering, Jim and Bonnie Harlow filed a lawsuit with six other adoptive couples. The lawsuit asked a federal court to overhaul the public adoption system in the state of Texas.

The Holy Spirit led me to contact them, and I was encouraged to learn that they were also Christians. Bonnie put me in contact with a nationally renowned psychologist, Dr. Foster Cline, who heads a clinic in Evergreen, Colorado. This clinic specializes in attachment disorders for children. Bonnie encouraged me and suggested that I retain an attorney for our protection. We ended our conversation with prayer for God's guidance and protection.

I learned that because of Julie's severe abuse and separations during her early years, she was never nurtured, and was never allowed to bond or form attachments to her parents or anyone. Unattached children manifest seventeen different symptoms, including lack of conscience, superficially charming, lack of ability to give and receive affection, extreme control problems, self-destructive behavior, lack of eye contact on parental terms, indiscriminate affection with strangers, lying about the obvious, frequent tantrums, cruelty to others and to pets, and more. Dr. Foster Cline of the Attachment Center in Evergreen, Colorado, has done pioneering work with these children. Dr. Ken Magid's book, *High Risk—Children Without a Conscience,* explores the issues surrounding the unattached child. Both these men and mental health professionals trained to work with unattached children strongly believe that therapy that is specialized to deal with abuse issues, attachment, and bonding is required to help these children. Traditional therapy does not work with unattached children. No amount of love and good parenting can reach these unattached children—they must have specialized treatment to be reached and helped. When unattached children are never reached, they become adults without a conscience. They then continue the cycle of abuse as they victimize others through abuse, sexual abuse, and other criminal activity and violence. The good news is that if these unattached children are treated at a young age, they can be helped and they can learn to bond with their parents.

I've met several parents over the years with adopted children out of state-run foster care. They experience such shame and guilt believing they have somehow failed these children. Their love and care have not helped them as they had hoped. Instead, their homes have become battlegrounds as the unattached children threaten family members and abuse other children in the homes. Only God can truly heal, deliver, and restore these wounded lambs. Not only do the emotional and physical issues need to be addressed, but also the spiritual aspects of these children.

I mailed letters to various government officials documenting our experience with the Department of Human Services (DHS). Little did I know that six months earlier, God had laid the groundwork that would later place one of those letters into the hands of the first lady of Hawaii. We had spent four hours together at a luncheon hosted by Protestant Women of the Chapel and enjoyed sharing about our husbands and children. When we parted, the first lady told me if I should ever need anything, to contact her. That's precisely what God led me to do after the children were taken. I felt impressed to call her and left a message with her secretary when I was told that she was out of town. A few days later, the first lady returned my call. She had read my letter and was alarmed that the Department of Human Services would remove the children from our home in such a traumatic way. I was amazed at the favor of God as she informed me that she placed my packet in the hands of her husband, the governor.

The local news reporter I'd previously spoken with called me on April 13, 1989, to find out what I had done about DHS's mistreatment of the children. He suggested that I contact two people in the legislature who might help. "Be careful," he cautioned. "This agency has a reputation of being vicious." I told him that DHS paid us money for taking care of the children, and he replied, "The check is a pay-off to keep you quiet. If you continue to speak out against this agency, they will slander you and say that your husband sexually abused Julie. They do it all the time."

It was incomprehensible for me to believe that people would go to such lengths to cover up gross mistakes.

According to a radio reporter, I opened a can of worms by filing a formal complaint against DHS. The director was looking down into a cesspool and doing everything she could to keep the lid on.

While sitting at my kitchen table one evening, seeking God's face, I heard Him ask, "Chandra, will you be a voice for My children and expose the injustices in the Department of Human Services?"

I wrestled and agonized over what God was calling me to do. Fear gripped me and I felt paralyzed by it. "But, Lord," I answered, "who am I to speak against this powerful organization that is capable of destroying lives? I'm just a homemaker. Who will listen to me?"

"Yes, child, but *who am I?* Greater is He that is in you than he that is in the world. All I need is your willing heart. Do you trust Me that I will be with you?"

I pondered over this. Wasn't it two years ago that I told the Lord how much I loved Him and that I would serve Him in any way He chose? That I would do anything for Him? I had meant it with all my heart. "Yes, Lord, I'm willing," I said. "I will speak out for Your children." Suddenly, fear fled, and God filled me with His love and peace.

The enemy returned to challenge my commitment to serve, tormenting me with his grip of fear. That same night, I was attacked in my sleep. In my dream I stood in a worship service and was called forward to lead worship. The congregation gathered around me to pray. Someone touched my head and prayed, "God has called you to accomplish this task." Suddenly, the power of the Holy Spirit came upon me. I fell prostrate on the floor as they continued to pray. Then I felt another presence nearby. I stood up and turned toward this person who was filled with evil. His eyes were full of hate and bore into mine. He sneered at me as if to say, "You have no power." I gasped and rebuked him in Jesus' name as he walked toward me. I called upon Jesus and His heavenly angels to surround and protect us. Overwhelmed with fear, I ran from this illuminated being coming toward me.

Abruptly, I awoke with my heart pounding. Petrified and unable to move, I whispered, "Jesus, help me. I need You. I need to hear Your voice. Speak to me through Your Word." I recited 2 Timothy 1:7: *"God hasn't given me a spirit of fear, but of power and of love and a sound mind."*

The presence of evil filled my bedroom. Quietly, I prayed for God's protection and for His angels to guard over my family. I felt His presence, and He gave me strength to walk into my children's rooms to pray over them.

I returned to my bedroom and looked at the clock. It was 3:30 a.m. I heard the Holy Spirit say, "I am here. Read Psalms 55 and 61." My heart quickened when I opened my Bible and read Psalm 61:1–4: *"Hear my cry, O God; Give heed to my prayer. From the end of the earth I call to You when my heart is faint; Lead me to the rock that is higher than I. For You have been a refuge for me, A tower of strength against the enemy. Let me dwell in Your tent forever; Let me take refuge in the shelter of Your wings."*

God lovingly showed me that He had protected me from the enemy. I was beginning to understand that I wasn't fighting against flesh and blood, but against powers and principalities in the spiritual realm.

TP finally rolled over and asked me, "What's the matter?"

I whispered, "I had a terrible nightmare. I'm okay now. Go back to sleep."

Moments later, I turned off my light and snuggled close to him. He must have sensed something because he put his arms around me and held me for a long time. When he called me from work the next morning and asked why I had trembled in his arms the night before, I told him about the dream. I was sure he wondered about the reality of it all. He'd later learn that these attacks from the enemy were very real. At that time, it was all new to me. Although I had been a Christian for eleven years, I hadn't even heard the term "spiritual warfare." Yet God had allowed me to experience it first hand in order to teach me His ways.

Months later, I had written confirmation of that warfare when a lady at my daughter's gymnastics class encouraged me to read *This Present Darkness* by Frank Peretti. She believed I was living his book, and I was.

CHAPTER 6

A Cry for the Children

Two weeks after the tragedy of the children's removal from our home, I contacted the state ombudsman, who is responsible for investigating complaints made by individuals against abuses by public officials. I informed him that we had received a letter from the Director of Human Services that addressed us only as foster parents, thus insinuating that we were never prospective adoptive parents. The number of government officials involved with our case astounded him. He informed me that there were no policies on adoption laws in the state of Hawaii. His voice trembled as he asked, "So, you're not satisfied with the letter?"

"No, we're not, because her letter is a lie. We had signed only the adoptive agreement and never signed a foster care document."

"What are you going to do with the check they gave you? What do you want out of all this?" he asked.

"I'm going to hang on to the check because I feel it's proof that something illegal went on," I replied. "Although

Julie was taken from my home, I still want to ensure she receives the help she needs in her new home."

I began to realize that the Director of Human Services was very powerful and everyone that I spoke with in Hawaii feared her. I needed outside help, so I called Focus on the Family, and they gave me a list of Christian attorneys who might be able to help. They suggested that I call John Whitehead at the Rutherford Institute. When I spoke with Mr. Whitehead, he suggested that I contact Gary Bauer at Family Research Council since I felt God leading me to write a letter to President George Bush. Mr. Bauer had worked on President Reagan's staff, and Mr. Whitehead thought he could better direct me in addressing this issue. I called and left a message for Gary Bauer, and it was a couple of days later when he returned my call. He encouraged me to speak out concerning the welfare of the children and write my letter to President Bush.

As I tucked Aaron into bed one night, he mentioned that I spent a lot of time on the computer. I hugged him and explained that God had called me to speak out against how the agency hurt Julie and Tommy. They could not speak for themselves, so I had to speak for them and be their voice. He was quiet for a moment as he contemplated what I said.

"Mommy, you're like Martin Luther King. He helped the black people." He paused and then said, "You know that lady in the movie *Gorillas in the Mist*? You're like her, too. She tried to help the gorillas, and her head got chopped off."

Aaron associated me with these people who tried to change things that were wrong and were killed. My heart ached to think that my son was worried that something terrible would happen to me. I prayed silently, asking God for wisdom in how to respond.

"Aaron, I can understand why you're worried about Mommy. But God is calling me to help these children, and I have to obey Him. Not everyone who does something good is killed. For example, Rosa Parks violated the law by sitting in the white section on a bus many years ago, and she's still alive. Moses was a man called by God to lead Israel out of Egyptian slavery, and God protected him. Therefore, God will protect me, too."

We prayed together for God's protection for our family and for Him to take care of Julie and Tommy. I hugged and kissed Aaron goodnight, and then sat at the side of his bed as he drifted off to sleep.

It wasn't too long before the unspeakable happened. My dear friend Debbie heard some disturbing news from an associate who was a social worker. Debbie was informed by this social worker that DHS had removed two adopted children from a black family that lived on Fort Shafter. According to DHS, this family complained that the girl had many behavior problems and believed she had been sexually abused before placement in their home. DHS claimed she hadn't shown any of these symptoms in the past. Therefore, the agency hastily removed the children, and the family was lucky that their birth children weren't also removed.

I sat speechless; I was watching the local reporter's warning unfold before my very eyes. Right there in the restaurant, Debbie and I bowed our heads and prayed that God would intervene. We came against this agency's wicked schemes, binding the demonic spirits in Jesus' name. I thanked God for providing this information to me prior to my upcoming meeting with a state representative.

On Wednesday morning, May 3, 1989 I prayed that the Lord would give me His words and open Representative Akaki's heart so that he would respond and help these children. The meeting with him went very well. He told me that I wasn't the first one to experience the abuse of power by DHS, but I was the first to have it so well documented. He wanted to know why I was pushing this issue. The Lord had already told me that I couldn't compromise.

I answered, "I'm here because something terribly wrong happened to innocent children. It's an injustice that my children were taken away from me, and there was nothing I could do to keep them. Not only has this agency traumatized the children we were adopting, but they have also traumatized my birth children. The Department of Human Services hides behind the disguise that they act in the 'best interest of the child.' But the truth is they protect themselves by covering their mistakes at the expense of destroying children's lives. Initially, this agency was designed to protect and help these children, not destroy them. It's time for this agency to be accountable for their wrongdoings. The main reason that I'm here is because these children do not have a voice. They can't speak for themselves and be heard. God's Word says, 'Learn to do good, seek justice, reprove the ruthless, and defend the orphan.' Foster children are the orphans of today. My God has given me strength to be here. He has sent me here to expose the injustices and speak the truth."

Rep. Akaki informed me that the letter I received from the governor's administrative director was written by DHS, and they did not investigate my complaint. He expressed his concern for the children and would talk with DHS.

God is so wonderful to equip us when He calls us to a task. Many times I sought God's wisdom through prayer. Some of my closest friends were confused and frightened about what had happened to Julie and Tommy. Some of them believed that I could have prevented DHS from taking the children if I had only tried harder. Several children in our neighborhood wanted to know if they could be taken away, too. During this time I withdrew from the community and grew closer to God and my family. So often, I felt alone.

I remember one sunny morning during my quiet time when I was feeling much like Elijah. I cried out to Jesus, pouring out my soul to Him: "Lord, I'm all alone. No one understands what You've called me to do, not even my husband. People ask me why I'm fighting this agency when it's apparent that the children aren't even coming back. Is there no one else who loves Your children and will fight for them?"

I was tired and afraid. Like Elijah, I felt my life had been threatened. In 1 Kings 19:10 NIV, Elijah says, *"I have been very zealous for the Lord God Almighty. The Israelites have rejected your covenant, broken down your altars, and put your prophets to death with the sword. I am the only one left, and now they are trying to kill me too."*

God's response to Elijah in verse 18 touched me deeply: *"Yet I will leave 7,000 in Israel, and all the knees that have not bowed to Baal and every mouth that has not kissed him."*

In other words, God was showing Elijah that he wasn't alone although he felt that way. God had seven thousand other praying saints. God always has a remnant. By no means can I compare myself with Elijah and the great commission that God gave him. But on a much smaller scale, I felt God telling me that I wasn't alone. He had others who would come alongside me to pray and support me. He confirmed this when I read Proverbs 24:6: *"For by wise guidance you will wage war, and in abundance of counselors there is victory."*

I had my Heavenly Father's assurance that I wasn't alone and there were other caring saints out there willing to help. I just hadn't found them yet.

God revealed to me that foster children in our country represent the orphans of today. They are constantly shuffled from one home to another and will never know the true meaning of love. We have a responsibility to defend the orphan according to God's Word in Isaiah 1:17, which reads: *"Learn to do good; seek justice, reprove the ruthless, defend the orphan, plead for the widow."*

In the spring of 1989, I was invited to attend a Protestant Women's Luncheon at Hickam Air Force Base. My friend encouraged me to go because the guest speaker was the legislative liaison for Concerned Women for America. Although I'd never heard of this organization, I sensed in my spirit that I was to attend. After the luncheon, I spoke with Paige Lawes, the guest speaker. As I told her about my nightmare experience, something wonderful began to take place. The burden I had carried now shifted onto her. She was like an angel sent by God to help. Paige shared the same love for Jesus and cared deeply for these children. Not only did God use Paige to open many doors for me in the state legislature, but also to introduce me to one of the most well respected attorney's on the island. I would later learn that seeking counsel protected me from further attacks from DHS.

I'll never forget the feeling I had when I walked into the attorney's office. I looked at my surroundings—the fine furniture, the accessories, and the view overlooking the Pacific Ocean—and I knew that God had given me favor. I was in awe of how God had arranged this meeting through Paige. There was no way that my husband and I could afford an attorney of this stature to represent us. When the meeting ended two hours later, he asked, "What is your goal? If you just want to get the children back, then DHS wouldn't hesitate one bit in placing those children back in your home. However, I see this as a bigger picture. The children have been gone now for two months. They are probably in a good home now because of all the attention the department is getting from numerous senators and representatives concerning your case. You've put pressure on them. There are a lot of Julies and Tommys out there, and I feel we could use this as a catalyst to change the system."

I paused for a moment to think before I responded. At this point, I knew in my heart that it wasn't God's will for the children to return to us. I agreed with him and felt that it would be more traumatic for the children if we uprooted them from their new family. But I still wanted to ensure that their new parents were informed of Julie's past so she could receive the necessary help.

I let the attorney know how much I appreciated him taking time out from his busy schedule to meet with me. I informed him that I needed to pray and ask God if He wanted us to pursue a class-action lawsuit.

CHAPTER 7

Opened Doors

During the first six months after the children were taken, I was compelled to contact and meet with every person or organization that I thought might have a sympathetic ear. I exerted pressure on myself that adversely affected my health and contributed to the pain on the right side of my abdomen. The pain was often unbearable. With this distraction, doubt sometimes crept in. God showed me in my quiet time that doubt was unbelief and it was sin. I confessed it and asked for His forgiveness. I learned how important it was for me to trust God and believe His Word.

He gave me Luke 21:15: *"For I will give you utterance and wisdom which none of your opponents will be able to resist or refute."* I heard the Spirit of the Lord say, *"Speak boldly in My name, and I will give you My words. TP will cover you, and I will speak to him."*

What comfort and encouragement I received from Him. I was not to worry about what I should say or do because God would give me His words and His wisdom! Looking back at that time, I believe God allowed the pain in my side and used it as a tool to slow me down. I didn't understand how to rest in Him, and I was just learning what it meant to wait on Him.

Although TP and I grew closer to the Lord, there was still a wedge between us. We had two separate opinions about the check the Department of Human Services sent to us and had some heated discussions over it. TP thought we should cash the check because of the expenses such as beds, clothes, and a new minivan. I felt that it was filthy money, a payoff to keep us quiet. If we cashed the check, we would be allowing them to cover up their mistakes. Now as I look back, I can see his viewpoint, but at the time I couldn't. TP also struggled with how strongly I felt God had called me to speak out about the injustice. He felt that we should just forget about the experience and move on. I spent many hours on my knees before the Lord because I saw how easily Satan could use this to destroy our marriage.

It was during those times I spent before the Lord that He gave me His Word to confirm that what I was doing was right in His sight and His will. Finally, I was able to share Ephesians 5:11–12 with TP: *"Do not participate in the unfruitful deeds of darkness, but instead even expose them; for it is disgraceful even to speak of the things which are done by them in secret."* I explained to TP how I believed that if we didn't speak out against this injustice, we were no better than the social worker and others carrying out their wicked schemes. God is telling us that when we see something wrong, we have a responsibility to expose it and take action.

Since I was unable to obtain information from the state ombudsman, I spent several hours at Hawaii's Supreme Court Law Library researching important information concerning state adoption laws and subsidies. I learned that, according to Hawaii's adoption laws, Julie and Tommy were children with special needs. They were considered hard to place because they were half black, siblings, and over the age of two. Based on these criteria, they were eligible for subsidies. The Lord revealed to me that many children and families were not receiving subsidies that they were entitled to. The initial thought that crossed my mind was "How many other children and families did not receive subsidies? Why didn't they receive it, and where was the money going?" When I addressed this issue with DHS officials, they became nervous. No one would explain why the children in the system were not receiving money due to them or where the money was being spent.

One evening in June 1989, while I was at work in the Army Reserves, the Holy Spirit impressed on my heart to speak with my supervisor about our experience with DHS. I was uncomfortable about what God wanted me to do. Again, I heard in my spirit, "Go tell Colonel Fisher about the children." Finally I resigned to what the Lord was saying and knocked on his door.

When I finished sharing my story with him, he asked, "Are you Catholic? It seems that you have a special calling."

"Although I was raised Catholic, I am a born again Christian," I answered.

He continued, "I want to help you. My wife and I attempted to adopt a child from Cambodia years ago, but she was killed when a plane crashed that was carrying her and many other orphans to the United States. We felt a tremendous loss. I can't imagine what loss you and your family suffered after having the children in your home. My wife and I suffered from that loss, and we didn't even have the child yet."

"Well, I thought you should know about our story from our view because when it comes out in the media, the state will have their side and it won't be the truth," I replied.

"What you're doing is very powerful. Laws are changed because of people like you. Sitting in front of senators and telling your story can change things. I want to help you, and I have several people I want you to meet with. Three people come to mind, and they were all at one time directors of Human Services. One is now a trustee of Bishop Estates. I suggest that you call the governor's secretary and tell her that I said to make an appointment to meet with both the administrative director and the governor. I encourage you to bring an attorney with you when you go."

I must have looked dumfounded, because he smiled at me and said, "I was the previous governor's right-hand man, so his secretary knows me. I also want you to meet with Senator Murphy who happens to be my neighbor. I'll call and let her know that you're going to call her."

I stood up and thanked him for all his help. I walked out of that meeting blown away by the Almighty God! In the past, I had wanted to quit my Army Reserve training many times, but TP insisted that I stay. I was so glad that I did after what came out of that meeting. I had no idea that Colonel Fisher had such influence.

I was astounded at how fast the doors flew open when I'd use his name when I contacted the list of people he gave me. I was encouraged by many to file a class-action lawsuit. Senator Murphy's secretary and others confirmed that DHS was corrupt, and maybe I was the one who was going to expose it.

By June, we no longer communicated with the director of Human Services because her letter to U.S. Representative Saiki was filled with inaccurate information. In fact, Representative Fred Hemmings, the minority leader of the House of Representatives, challenged the inaccuracies of her letter by writing:

The welfare of the children should be first and foremost. Would it be possible for a third party, other than someone on your payroll, a guardian ad litem, or a child psychologist to visit the children at their new home? I believe there are some severe communication problems regarding the children. The problems include the emotional condition of Julie, who seemed to be locked up in a room at her prior home under the guise of childproofing, the DHS "hold status" that was contradicted when the children were abruptly removed from the Moyer's home, and additional particulars. These issues should be clarified.

Why was the state so hasty in producing a check of $1,000+ for the Moyers when it appears they didn't request or cash it? Was this a unilateral action on the part of the State? I hate to be so cynical, but I hope this was not an effort to pay the Moyers off in hopes they would disappear. As a legislator, I am very cognizant of social worker burnout and of the difficulty the State is having taking care of the less fortunate in our society. The problems seem to be escalating in spite of the huge budget and dramatically increased resources. First and foremost, our concerns should be focused on the welfare of the children, not the system.

About this same time, a local reporter for the *Honolulu Star Bulletin* came to my home to write our story. She thought we had an incredible story and also wanted to take pictures for the article. Helen felt that the children could still be in foster care.

She said, "You are articulate and intelligent; that is what's frightening DHS. They tried paying you off and it didn't work. Then they started a slanderous rumor about you and that backfired. They just don't know what to do about you. Most people give up, and you haven't yet. It will take me some time to track all the people involved, especially since they avoid me when I call." I thanked her for her compassion toward the children and any help she could give to us.

In July I was invited to speak at Concerned Women for America in Honolulu. I addressed the adoption problems that plague the state. After the meeting, a woman approached me who had recently come from the mainland and was very active in right-to-life issues. She cautioned me to be very careful with the government here in Hawaii because they can be very mean. "They could take your children, so be careful," she warned. Fear was always lurking around, and it was ready to pounce on me again after her statement. I continually had to fight against the spirit of fear through prayer.

Finally, when I met with the TV News reporter who had tracked my story over several months, I learned how powerful these men were that I had met.

"I'm just amazed at all the people you have spoken with. How did you get in the door to meet these men?" he asked.

"My supervisor, Bob Fisher, suggested that I contact them," I answered.

Astounded, he said, "Your boss is Bob Fisher? He's a man of great influence. Do you realize that you have talked to the most powerful people on this island? I can't even reach these people. You've spoken with the shakers and makers of the state of Hawaii. That's incredible! How did you do it?"

I replied, "I believe that God opened these doors so that I could speak on behalf of His children."

Now I was truly amazed. That God had brought me before leaders in the state government was unthinkable to me. In the past, politics and government weren't subjects I found particularly interesting. I admit that I was quite ignorant about how our government worked, and to some degree I still am!

TP and I finally met with the governor's administrative director. He informed us that he had received a letter from an attorney saying that the children were all right. I knew the letter was from the children's guardian who was afraid of losing her job, so she wasn't going to make waves. We informed the administrative director that we weren't happy about DHS and felt that our questions had not been satisfied.

Each time someone from the legislature would suggest a

course of action, I'd take it before the Lord. I needed to hear from Him and how He wanted us to proceed. Although many people told me to file a class-action lawsuit, the Lord never led me in that direction. I sensed that God had appointed someone else who permanently resided on the island to do that, and I would support him or her with our testimony. Two years later, I would receive a call from Lin Costa asking us to join her and others in a class-action lawsuit against the state of Hawaii. Child Protective Services falsely accused Lin and her husband of child abuse and took their daughter. Consequently, their daughter was placed in foster care for three years and was sexually abused while living in that foster home.

CHAPTER 8

Truth Exposed

On September 12, 1989, our story was featured on the front page of the *Honolulu Star Bulletin*. It was incorporated into a three-part series about the problems that plague the Department of Human Services. A few days later, I received a call from a lady in Virginia Beach, Virginia. She bought a newspaper the day she left Hawaii and read our story on her flight home. Rhonda explained, "Our family is going through a nightmare experience with DHS. My nephew was placed in foster care, and we can't get him out of the system to adopt him. I feel your article is an answer to prayer, and we believe that there is a money scam behind this entire mess."

We prayed for her nephew's protection and for the Lord's guidance and wisdom. I also received a call later from Rhonda's sister, saying, "We have spent over $10,000 in attorneys' fees in trying to get Michael. Dr. Chung told us that it would be too disruptive to move him from his foster home. We want to raise Michael with his sister who is living with us already."

This contradicted Dr. Chung's statement to us concerning keeping Julie and Tommy together. We were told that they keep siblings together, and that is why the state removed both children from our home. Yet, they weren't placing Michael with his full-blooded sister!

During the months of October and September 1989, several radio broadcasters interviewed me. By November, several organizations supported my efforts to reform the adoption and foster care systems and a press conference was held at the state capitol.

Finally, after eight months of avoiding me, I received a call from Senator Murphy's secretary to schedule an appointment. Senator Murphy apologized for not meeting with me sooner. She heard that I was suing the state, so she had to be careful in her position. She also felt that nothing in the system would change unless someone files a class-action suit. During the course of our meeting, Senator Murphy said, "You should be able to write a book about your experience with the state." I didn't share with her that the Lord had already called me to write a book about His silent lambs.

In spite of all the people I met with, I still felt very discouraged because I saw no immediate results from my efforts to help these children. The pain and heartbreak of not protecting them was a heavy burden to bear. Nothing had turned out like I had hoped. The children weren't returned as I had initially thought, and I still didn't know if they were out of foster care. The system was accountable to no one, not even to the state legislature. During those months, I heard heart-wrenching stories of other families and children torn apart by this agency that was supposedly designed to protect children.

I was tired of all the lies the agency spread about us. The reason given for the children being removed from our home shifted like the wind. Initially, we were told by DHS that the children's placement was a mismatch and therefore not workable. Next, we received a letter from the director addressing us as foster parents, never acknowledging us as prospective adoptive parents. Finally, Senator Koki who questioned DHS on our behalf informed me that the children were removed because we were a military family due to leave the island soon. Where was the integrity in this system?

Senator Koki asked me to testify at a hearing held by the Human Services Committee in February 1990. This would be my last assignment from the Lord before leaving the island. What I witnessed at the hearing disturbed me. After the director of Human Services delivered her speech, I challenged her statement that the department had a grievance committee established for complaints. Senator Murphy nervously interrupted me as I presented my testimony before the Human Services Committee. I realized then that the Department of Human Services controlled that hearing, and the senator was only a puppet for the department.

A year after the children's removal and a couple of weeks before we left Hawaii in May 1990, I called the children's previous foster mother. She informed me that the children's new adoptive mother was primarily concerned that the judge would not rule to finalize the adoption. Apparently it took eleven months to finalize. I was grateful to hear that a Navy military family adopted Julie and

Tommy. I hung up the phone and cried bitter tears, thanking God for taking them out of the foster care system and placing them in a military family.

A few days before moving to our next assignment, I sat on a friend's bench overlooking the Pacific Ocean. I saw the awesome beauty of God as I gazed into that vast ocean. I reflected upon the past few weeks of struggling to let go of this battle because the heavy burden of not protecting Julie and Tommy weighed on me the entire year. With God's grace I was able to release the burden, and now I was free to move on. As I sat resting in His presence, I pondered a prophetic word I had received a year and half earlier, only a few months before Julie and Tommy entered our lives: "God's hand is on you and so is the anointing of the Holy Spirit. Out of all the women in this room, you are very instrumental in making things happen. I can see the Holy Spirit's aura around you. You have a humble spirit, yet you are a leader. God is calling you in the area of government. You will speak with people in high positions. You will be placed in positions to bridge gaps and bring people together. You are a leader and will lead leaders."

I wept profusely as the power of the Holy Spirit came upon me. It was a divine and supernatural encounter that I had never before experienced. In the past, I had even doubted the prophetic gift. I couldn't get home fast enough to get on my knees before the Lord and question Him about what all this meant. "Called to the area of government, when I have no interest in it?" I thought. "How will this happen? I'm a wife and mother who is about to adopt two children, which means a total of four kids to raise. Lord, this will probably happen twenty years from now. Although I don't understand, Lord, I believe You because I know that it was You who spoke to me. I will trust You even though I can't see how this will ever come to pass."

Yet, that's where I found myself eight months later, speaking out on behalf of God's children before the state legislature. TP felt that this was only the beginning of the prophecy. *"And you shall even be brought before governors and kings for My sake, as a testimony to them and to the Gentiles. But when they deliver you up, do not become anxious about how or what you will speak; for it shall be given you in that hour what you are to speak. For it is not you who speak, but it is the Spirit of your Father who speaks in you."* Matthew 10:18-20

CHAPTER 9

A Promise Fulfilled

After our move to Ft. Leavenworth, Kansas, the Lord continued to show me His sovereignty. God graciously blessed us with another baby. We adopted Micah on December 5, 1990, through a private adoption agency. He is now truly a part of our family, a privilege that we were denied with Julie and Tommy. In the fall of 1990, as I read Genesis 50 about Joseph's reunion with his family, the Lord revealed to me that I would see Julie and Tommy again. When Joseph's brothers sold him into slavery, they meant evil against him, but God meant it for good so that he would preserve many people during the famine. It took years before Joseph saw the good in what God allowed to happen to him. I penned in my journal:

> I praise You, dear Father. You are mighty and all-powerful. The social worker meant evil against us, but You meant it for good and to bring about a result in the future we're unable to see now.

Although it took Joseph many years before he saw the good in what the Lord allowed to happen to him, he continued to rely on the Lord. Jesus, I praise You that You have allowed evil to happen to me to bring about good so that You are glorified. You have prepared our hearts for Micah through this painful experience. He is such a blessing and a bundle of joy. I praise You for Your greatness and infinite wisdom. Although Jacob lost his son Joseph, God brought him back in his old age. Lord, I believe that You will bring Julie and Tommy back into our lives in the future. I am overwhelmed by Your love for us. Thank You for Your words of truth.

Five months after this entry, I spoke with my old neighbor Ann, who had moved to Alabama. I shared how God revealed to me that I would see the children again. Ann excitedly told me that she had met a nice lady at a park near her home. This woman had recently moved from Honolulu, Hawaii, and was a social worker. Ann learned that she was assigned to Julie and Tommy's case after they were removed from our home. She informed Ann that the children's adoption was finalized and they were living with a military family in the states. I rejoiced as I hung up the phone. If the Lord could arrange a meeting like that in Alabama, then it was possible for Him to bring the children back into our lives in His timing!

"And we know that God causes all things to work together for good to those who love God, to those who are

called according to His purpose." What revelations God gave me in reading Romans 8:28. Even when ugly, painful things happen in our lives, God is faithful to work them for our good. Was God sovereign when the social worker took Julie and Tommy from our home? Yes, God is still on the throne, but He gives free will to men. I've often cried out to God, "Why, Lord? What good can come out of all this suffering?"

As I reflect back, I've come to understand that God called us to take those children into our home to love them, but He never told us what the outcome would be. If He had told me in advance what we would have to walk through in opening our home and hearts to these children, I know I probably would have said, "Lord, I love You, but find someone else who will make that sacrifice." Was I willing to experience suffering and pain to help others and make their lives better? No, I don't think so, because by human nature I believe that we avoid pain and suffering at all cost. Apart from God, I'm a selfish and self-centered human being.

On the contrary, "God so loved the world, that He gave his one and only Son, that whosoever believes in Him shall not perish, but have eternal life" (John 3:16). Jesus willingly laid down His life for humanity by dying on the cross for our sins. He took our sins upon Himself and became sin for us so that we might become the righteousness of God. If we truly want to know Christ and the power of His resurrection, we must be willing to share in His suffering, becoming like Him in His death. That means laying down our lives, our self-centeredness, and our ambitions to help children in need.

I had to trust that God was directing all things according to His purposes, even when I didn't understand why the events happened as they did. His Word says, *"Trust in the Lord with all your heart, and do not lean on your own understanding. In all your ways acknowledge Him, and He will make your paths straight"* (Proverbs 3:5–6). I was truly learning to trust and rely on Him.

A year after our move to Colorado Springs in April of 1992, I was praying in the Spirit while changing Micah's diaper. I heard the Holy Spirit say, "It's time to write to Jean Chase because I'm sending you to Washington, D.C., to speak with certain people." I had previously met Jean four years earlier at the Religious Freedom Conference while living in Hawaii. We had dinner together, and I had the opportunity to share our story about the children. Jean was very interested in our situation and asked me to send her all of my newspaper articles. She believed that God was using me and wanted to help any way she could. Handing me her address, Jean said, "Feel free to call me if you need any help, because I believe God's taking you places." At that time Jean was on the board of Concerned Women for America.

The Lord gave me the verse in Psalm 82:3–4 (NIV) and began to speak to me again about His children: *"Defend the cause of the weak and the fatherless; maintain the rights of the poor and oppressed. Rescue the weak and needy; deliver them from the hand of the wicked."* I knew that I must obey Him and go to Washington.

I wrote to Jean, and a few months later we spoke on the telephone. She suggested that I speak with several people within Concerned Women for America who could help steer me in the right direction. This organization was both supportive and helpful. I was referred to Free Congress

Foundation because it provides a platform for Christian organizations to meet and address various issues. In August, I spoke with the coordinator for the monthly forum, and he was very interested in my views concerning government intrusion in families. I asked if I could attend one of their meetings. I was shocked when he extended me an invitation to speak at their next meeting to present my issue of concern.

Two weeks later, I flew out to Washington, D.C. I received a warm welcome at Free Congress Foundation, and the forum went very well. Presenting this issue before this organization provided a platform for me to meet with other leaders from organizations such as Traditional Values Coalition and Family Research Council, to name a few. After returning home to Colorado Springs, I began to receive letters from parents throughout the United States who had experienced horrendous abuse at the hands of various state Child Protective Services (CPS).

Free Congress referred my name to many people. One individual happened to work for Focus on the Family in the public policy division. I was introduced to the director of public policy and met with him on several occasions. I was invited to attend the Family Policy Council Board Conference in February 1993.

About this same time, I started meeting with local organizations in Colorado Springs to establish a network on the national level that would expose the abuse and corruption within CPS and work to change current laws affecting families. A few months after these meetings began, everything came to a screeching halt. At thirty-seven years of age, the secret of my past had invaded my present world and I could no longer run from it. Emotionally depleted, I sought Godly counsel as I faced the truth about my own childhood trauma. With this mountain of pain looming before me, I had to lay everything aside so that God could heal me. At the time, I had no idea of the magnitude of the problems that plague America's Child Protective Services. To be an effective witness, I would need to be healed before I could move forward on this mission.

CHAPTER 10

A National Crisis

The Child Protection System is currently set up to move children from one home to another instead of trying to find permanent placement. If care providers are so bold as to speak out on behalf of the children when they see Child Protective Services doing something wrong as we did, they could be subject to false accusations of child abuse. According to the president of the National Committee for Adoption in Washington, D.C., going public protected us from brutal attacks by DHS.

Currently there are 127,000 foster children like Julie and Tommy who no longer live with their parents and have been declared by the courts as free to be adopted, but often languish for months or even years in state-run, state-funded substitute care. According to the U.S. Department of Health and Human Services AFCARS, 568,000 children—none eligible for adoption—can be found in government foster homes, group homes, and shelters. Many are kept in state custody due to absentee parents clinging to their legal rights.[1]

America spends over $15 billion a year on foster care and adoption services through public agencies. The problem with foster care is not the level of government spending; it is the structure of that spending. I believe that to create a more efficient system, we must draw on private and faith-based adoption agencies. Government must get out of the business of parenting. Children need families, and government cannot be a substitute for family.

In her book, *Transforming America from the Inside Out*, Kay Coles James writes: "The government has not yet invented a program, a piece of legislation, or a department that can give hope to a disconnected urban youth, that can help a husband love his wife, that can teach a child honesty and integrity, or that can bring youth face to face with the person of Christ. That is because such a program doesn't exist. The only place where such a program can happen is in our homes, in our schools, and in our churches."

As much as the government would like society to believe that they know what's best for our children. The government cannot raise our children. The state cannot hug children and tuck them into bed at night. God clearly delegates the responsibility of rearing, protecting, nurturing, and caring of a child to parents, not to the government. God's Word says that parents are to *"train up a child in the way he should go, even when he is old, he will not depart from it"* (Proverbs 22:6). *And, fathers, do not provoke your children to anger; but bring them up in the discipline and instruction of the Lord"* (Ephesians 6: 4). In many ways, we as parents have relinquished our role of parenting to the schools and the government. Now we are suffering the consequences. I believe the community has an important responsibility to fortify and support the family unit.

In our social-work schools, counseling centers, and government-funded research, the culture of victimization insists that the most despicable behavior by abusive parents has its causes in economics, racism, broken homes—anything but the consciences and moral choices of men and women.[2] But the truth is that the moral fabric of our society is unraveling at an accelerated pace because of our spiritual condition. We have chosen as a nation to turn away from God's truths to walk in our own ways. Our culture says that if it feels good, do it. As a result, the United States is facing a social crisis: fatherless children. As a nation, the U.S. has the highest teenage pregnancy rate of all developed countries.

As a result of this moral decline, physical, sexual and emotional abuse has become a very serious problem in our society. Some children are in danger of being harmed by severely abusive parents, and those children should be removed immediately from their parents' homes. Unfortunately, what happens is that these children are often returned to their parents, only to be abused again. In these situations, parental rights should be terminated so that these children can be free to be adopted.

On the flip side of this issue are the thousands of parents who are falsely accused of child abuse. Our encounter with social services when they spitefully intimidated us by falsely accusing us of sexually abusing Julie was a harrowing one. According to Richard Wexler, the executive director of the National Coalition of Child Protection Reform, it is estimated that over one million people are falsely accused of child abuse every year in this country. I've corresponded with many parents who have suffered the trauma of having their children taken away due to false accusations.

The Jones family is one of thousands of families who have experienced severe heartache and devastation at the hands of a child welfare agency. Lin's eight-year-old daughter Kelly was playing with friends one day after school. A male stranger abducted Kelly and sexually molested her. He threatened to kill Kelly and her parents unless she told the police that her parents were the ones who abused her. Although Kelly was afraid, she refused to comply. The man grabbed her by the arms and shook her violently, and repeated his threats. Kelly begged him, "Please don't hurt me, but I'm still not going to tell." The man elicited his wife who accompanied Kelly to the police station to make sure a police report was generated naming the parents as the abusers. The lady identified herself as a friend of the family. Kelly was then transferred to state Child Protective Services and placed in a foster home, where she was abused. Three years and $8,000 later, the Jones' finally got their daughter back, traumatized under the guise of her best interest.

In my opinion, this is the abuse of families in the name of child protection, and it has shown an alarming rate of growth in the last decade. Often children are removed from their families prematurely or unnecessarily because federal aid formulas give states a strong financial incentive to do so rather than provide services to keep families together. Currently there are incentives to keep children in foster care and incentives to find adoptive homes. However, there are no incentives to keep children in their own homes or return them. This poses a serious dilemma. CPS is more likely to lean toward placing children in foster care or adoptive families rather than return them to their own homes because of the financial incentive they will receive.

Although the problem of child abuse is serious and real, the first step toward viable solutions is to try to get honest facts. What do the numbers really mean? When news stories report that over three million children are abused in this country, we often think of children severely abused by their parents. The fact is that two-thirds of those reports are false. Nationwide, at least fifty-six percent of "substantiated" child abuse cases involve allegations of neglect, not abuse. Most children come into foster care due to neglect, which can be extremely serious. It can mean a parent deliberately starving a child or leaving the child alone for days at a time. But far more often, it means the child is hungry because the food stamps ran out or is left alone because his mother is terrified of being sanctioned off the welfare rolls for not showing up at her make-work job. Florida's Department of Children and Families (DCF) defines neglect as "a caregiver's failure or omission to provide a child with the care, supervision, and services necessary to maintain the child's physical and mental health, including, but not limited to, food, nutrition, clothing, shelter, supervision, medicine, and medical services." By that definition, almost any poor family, at some time or other, could be caught in DCF's web.[3]

I've spoken with parents who had their children taken from them solely because they were poor. How can we punish loving parents whose only crime is poverty? So often family poverty is confused with neglect. Many times I felt that Julie and Tommy would have been better off living in a car with their mother than enduring the abusive treatment they had received through Social Services. The intervention that they received from this system caused them more harm than good. Wouldn't it have been more effective for the state to provide ready cash for rent subsidy?

What was distressing to us was the lack of respect DHS had toward the role of parents as the primary responsible source for their children's growth and development. There was no respect for the integrity of the family. It should neither be the goal nor the function of federal, state, or local government to usurp the role of parents, yet that is precisely what we encountered at the hands of Child Protective Services (CPS).

Before you form the opinion that I'm against social workers, I want to assure you that I am not. I believe that many are sincere and want to help children. However, caseworkers are often in their early twenties and just out of college and are therefore lacking the personal experience of raising children themselves. The little training they have received has taught them that any parent is a potential abuser, that most parents don't really know what they're doing, and that all parents are suspect. They learn that spanking is always wrong and warrants the removal of children.[4]

Caseworkers carry heavy loads that make it humanly impossible to keep track of children. The average caseworker's load is forty to sixty children. According to the Child Welfare League of America, the professional standard is seventeen per caseworker.[5] Those who care tend to suffer burnout because the system is currently designed to fail. Is there any surprise that the annual turnover rate of workers is as high as seventy percent in some areas?

Currently in their pursuit to rescue every child, this agency is destroying innocent families. It's time for CPS to come to terms with the fact that they cannot prevent all child abuse. But their effectiveness can be greatly increased by improving the ability of agencies to help their clients by reducing caseloads, improving training of case workers and funding more intensive family preservation programs.

Initially, when our family was rocked by this tragedy, I thought that this problem was unique to the state of Hawaii. However, after living in five different states over the past twelve years, I've learned that the Child Protection System is in a national crisis. Unfortunately, little has changed and it appears that the problem has only escalated. For example, Rilya Wilson, a five-year-old girl living in foster care in Florida, disappeared for more than a year before social services was even aware that she was missing. The foster parent, who has twice been convicted on fraud and theft charges, claims she gave Rilya to a caseworker with the state Department of Children and Families in January 2001. Rilya's caseworker was accused of falsifying monthly visit reports. Unfortunately, mishandled cases, files hidden to cover up shoddy work, and dishonesty in the system is not rare. Rilya is one of hundreds of children who have been lost by Florida's child-welfare system.[6] How many children are missing across this nation and not accounted for in this system?

In June 2002, Logan Marr's foster mother was found guilty of wrapping the five-year-old's body with forty-two feet of duct tape during a "timeout," causing the little girl to suffocate. Six weeks before she was killed, Logan was visiting her birth mother and complained that her foster mother was hurting her. Logan is heard saying on videotape, "She did this to me and I cried 'cause it hurts me." There was no immediate investigation by Maine's child welfare agency despite this information.

The state child welfare agencies hold a double standard for themselves. They often turn a blind eye to a foster parent's convicted charges of theft and turn a deaf ear to a child's cry of being abused by a foster parent. It appears that the state is quick to remove children from biological parents for accusations of child abuse, often with little proof. Yet, when abuse occurs in foster homes under state supervision, the abuse is grossly ignored. In the case of adoption, whether through private or public adoption agencies, would-be parents must undergo a home study. Private or other faith-based adoption agencies typically emphasize tough standards of behavior. This is not so for state agencies. In many states, adults who fail an adoption home study can become foster parents. Unfit to serve as legal adoptive parents, these adults are then paid to raise children in state care.

Before our experience with Hawaii's state human services, I was like so many trusting Americans. I truly believed that the child welfare agency in our nation was one of integrity that protected children from abusive parents, but I've learned otherwise. The tragedy is that the American public has been misled to believe that they are doing a noble thing when they call Child Protection Services to report possible child abuse. CPS is itself an overburdened agency that is abusing and losing children. Though it may be well intentioned, impersonal government intervention doesn't always alleviate the suffering of abused and neglected children. Why continue to pour more money into a corrupt child welfare system that is so damaging to vulnerable children? There are no easy solutions. However, states like Michigan, where two-thirds of foster care management is privatized, private providers spend less per child yet have achieved better social worker-to-child ratios than those of state-run agencies. Michigan has the largest family preservation program in America and also has an outstanding record for getting foster children adopted.

Adoption is, in fact, the ultimate form of privatization: wresting authority over children's lives from the state and allowing children to be free, to be raised not by government but by parents. We must reform, state by state, our system of transferring parental rights from the government, which can never be a parent, to parents who are eager and able to bring these children into their hearts and lives.[7]

CHAPTER 11

System Reform

One topic few people like to address is the issue of failed adoptions. Some people estimate, up to half of all the adoptions in America fail, resulting in the children leaving their "forever families" only to return to foster care and/or to other adoptive parents. Attachment disorders are emerging as the chief cause of fostering and adoption breakdowns, according to David Howe, professor of social work at the University of East Anglia, England. The irony is that adoptive and foster parents are frequently given advice that a loving and stable home can compensate for primary losses. Yet in reality, traumatized children can traumatize an entire family, leaving caregivers struggling in their ignorance and desperation, blaming themselves and often giving up all together.[8]

Many families adopting children out of foster care are unprepared to raise a special needs or high risk child. Too often adoptive parents are told, "All this child needs is love and everything will be fine." This is not true. Like so many other families adopting foster children, we found ourselves in tragic situations that we were unprepared to handle. Because many families are unprepared to raise a high risk or special needs child resources are drained and great stress is placed on the family. I believe the reason why many adoptions aren't working is because the parents have had no one to help them. To successfully raise these children, the adoptive families need additional resources and support. Several organizations are recognizing this need and implementing innovative means to accomplish this.

Brenda Krause Eheart, a University of Illinois professor of sociology, founded Generations of Hope and Hope Meadows. Hope Meadows is a planned community located on a former military training base in Rantoul, Illinois, where foster and adoptive families, children and older adults live together and care for each other. The intergenerational neighborhood provides ongoing support to families adopting those foster children who are among the most difficult to place in nurturing, permanent homes. In direct contrast with traditional foster-care programs, Generations of Hope has created a place where adoptive families can get the support and information they need and be nurtured emotionally, intellectually and financially. The kids who wind up at Hope are among the most wounded the child-welfare system sees, and the ones it tends to serve the least well. Hope has had a remarkable success. Overtime, seventy-five children referred by the Illinois Department of Children and Family Services have moved to Hope. Statically, 90 percent of them were able to leave the foster care system, most by being adopted, some by returning to their birth families. Hope dramatically improves a child's chances of escaping the foster care system and of finding a loving and permanent home, a place where he or she really does belong and Hope does this for half the cost.[9]

The Attachment Center at Evergreen, Colorado is an internationally recognized treatment and training program. A dedicated team of professionals and therapeutic families work to help families with adoptive or foster children work through early abuse and emerge on the other side into a healthy, loving lifestyle. They have successfully treated hundreds of children with attachment disorder since 1972.

Homebuilders Family Preservation program determines those families in which children could remain in their homes or be returned home safely. They also determine the provision of services needed to ensure that safety. The intervention begins when the family is in crisis and is designed for families whose children otherwise face immediate removal to foster care. Although the interventions is short, usually four to six weeks it's extremely intense. The Homebuilders model requires that the family be linked to less intensive support after the intervention to maintain the gains made by the family. Homebuilders family preservation program was hired by one Washington State agency to preserve adoptive families. Intensive family preservation programs have a better record of safety than foster care. Since 1982, the original Homebuilders has served 12,000 families. No child has ever died during a Homebuilders intervention, and only one child has ever died afterwards.[10]

Many of the organizations dealing with these precious children address only the physical, intellectual, and emotional needs. But for complete healing to occur, God needs to heal their spirits. God calls His church to be the family for orphans according to James 1:27 NIV: *"Religion that God our Father accepts as pure and faultless is this: to look after orphans and widows in their distress and to keep oneself from being polluted by the world."* The church has a mandate from God to take care of the orphans, but has neglected its responsibilities for too long. It is time for the church to arise and take action to tend to these children in foster care and provide support for adoptive families. The church has the ability to address the spiritual aspects of these children's lives.

Our Father in heaven loves these orphaned children very much. They are precious to Him, and He is concerned about them. Psalm 72:12–14 NIV: *"For he will deliver the needy who cry out, the afflicted who have no one to help. He will take pity on the weak and the needy and save the needy from death. He will rescue them from oppression and violence, for precious is their blood in his sight."*

Reform is needed in the following areas. First, we must ensure that abused children receive the immediate, emergency protection to which they are entitled and not be returned into abusive homes. To effectively do this, we must prevent non-abusive parents from forced contact with a system whose services are unwanted and unneeded, thus unclogging the system of children that don't belong there. This frees resources so they can be spent in much more productive ways in helping abused children. We must provide a higher level of due process protection for these families and children that do come into contact with the system.[11]

Secondly, increased accountability for caseworkers and

their supervisors is critical to ensure the welfare of hurting children. Corruption is rampant throughout the system because of the cloak of secrecy that allows this system to hide. Evidence shows that secrecy protects social workers from being held accountable for their actions. Unlimited power breeds unlimited abuse.

Third, raise standards for licensing of foster parents. By maintaining a separate set of standards for foster parents from those of adoptive parents, we are saying to half a million children that it is not important where they spend the most formative years of their lives. A child is more than twice as likely to die of abuse in foster care than in the general population according to national data on child abuse fatalities.

Fourth, reverse financial incentives that encourage foster care and discourage programs to keep children out of foster care. The federal government spends at least eight times more on foster care than on services to keep families together. Currently, there are no incentives to keep children in their homes or return them.

Fifth, provide information, support services, and resources for those families adopting hard-to-place kids and those suffering from attachment disorders.

Sixth, narrow the definition of neglect to make it more difficult to confuse neglect with poverty.

Seventh, improve training and experience requirements for CPS workers.

These are only a few ways in which the system can be reformed. My story is not the only one that shows how the system is broken and is failing our most vulnerable citizens.

Many stories are out there, and we read about them in newspapers every day. We hear about them from friends, family, and even strangers. Where can one turn to for help and assistance? There are several resources listed in the back of this book that may help you in your search.

CHAPTER 12

Healing Grace

U naware of my own childhood trauma at the time, I was driven to defend Julie to the point of exhaustion. I so identified with Julie that I was willing to fight Hawaii's Department of Human Services to try and protect her. I would learn a few years later that my own abusive past had fueled my passion to defend Julie. Incredibly, God used this tragedy with these children to uncover repressed memories of sexual and ritual abuse in my own life. In speaking out for Julie, I found my voice—a voice that shouts injustice, a voice that shouts terror, a voice that shouts pain, agony, and despair, a voice heard always by our Heavenly Father. We are the children of silent cries and unseen tears.

In experiencing my heavenly Father's love, I received healing from the pain of past sexual and ritual abuse. I thank God for good counselors, because He blessed me with a wonderful Christian counselor who loved and encouraged me when I thought I couldn't go on. But it was the healing power of His Son, Jesus Christ that cleansed me from the effects of guilt and shame associated from my abuse. I want to encourage others who have been abused physically, emotionally, or sexually that there is a balm in Gilead who desires to take all your pain, and His name is Jesus. He is a miracle-working God who loves you with an everlasting love. His desire is to heal your shattered heart, restore you, and bring you into wholeness and oneness with Him.

You may be hurting now as you're reading this book. Jesus wants to touch you right now where you are. Maybe you grew up in the foster care system and feel that you don't belong anywhere because you were bounced around from one house to another. God's Word says that He will never leave you nor forsake you, and He sets the lonely in families. You might be a social worker who feels guilty about some of the decisions you have made concerning the children under your care. God says that if you confess your sins, He is faithful and just to forgive you of your sins and cleanse you from all unrighteousness.

Perhaps you are a parent or caretaker who has perpetrated abuse and is serving time in prison. Love covers a multitude of sin. God demonstrates His own love for us in this: while we were still sinners, Christ died for us.

Whatever condition you are in, Jesus is waiting to save, heal, forgive, and restore you. I cannot keep to myself what God did for me, but I am compelled to share with you. He set me free from my prison of pain, my dungeon of shame, and shackles of guilt. What He did for me He desires to do for you! Beloved, our heavenly Father loves you and wants to bring you out of your pit of darkness and into His marvelous light. Will you allow Him to wrap His arms of love around you to comfort you? Will you pray this prayer from your heart to accept Jesus and begin your journey to wholeness?

Heavenly Father, I come to You because I'm hurting and I need You. I'm tired of doing things my own way and surrender my life to You. I believe You have a wonderful plan for my life. I thank you for loving me and sending your son to die on the cross for my sins. Right now I repent of all my sins and ask that You forgive me. Jesus I ask you to come into my heart and be Lord of my life. Thank you for saving me now in Jesus' name, Amen.

If you have asked Jesus to come into your heart, something incredible just happened. Your spirit has come alive and you are now reconciled to God. He not only wants to be your Savior and Lord, but your friend. It's an amazing thing that a powerful God desires to have a personal relationship with you. As a child of God you have received the gift of the Holy Spirit (Acts 2:38, 8:15) and will spend eternity in heaven. Jesus says to his disciples in John 14:15 NIV, *"If you love me, you will obey what I command. And I will ask the Father, and he will give you another Counselor to be with you forever-the Spirit of truth. The world cannot accept him, because it neither sees him nor knows him. But you know him for he lives with you and will be in you. I will not leave you as orphans; I will come to you.*

Welcome to the family of God! I encourage you to begin reading the Bible, God's word. If you don't already have a church, I pray that the Holy Spirit will lead you to a loving body of believers who can help you grow in the faith as you begin this new life.

God sets the lonely in families. (Psalm 68:6 NIV)

Suggested Resources

1. National Coalition for Child Protection Reform
   53 Skyhill Road, Suite 202
   Alexandria, VA 22314
   www.nccpr.org
   Phone/Fax: (703) 212–2006
   e-mail: NCCPR@AOL.COM

2. Family Research Council
   801 G Street, NW
   Washington, DC 20001
   Phone: (202) 393–2100

3. A Generation of Hope
   1530 Fairway Drive
   Rantoul, IL 61866
   (217) 893–4673
   www.generationsofhope.org

4. Home School Legal Defense Association
    P.O. Box 3000
    Purceville, VA 20134-9000
    (540) 338-5600

5. National Adoption Information Clearinghouse
    330 C Street, SW
    Washington, DC 20447
    Phone: (703) 352–3488 or (888) 251–0075
    naic@calib.com

6. The Attachment Center at Evergreen
    P.O. Box 2764
    Evergreen, CO 80437-2764
    (303) 674-1910
    www.attachmentcenter.org

7. (NASVO) National Association of State VOCAL
    Organizations Inc.
    1-800-745-8778
    www.nasvo.org

8. VOCAL NY Inc.
    P.O. Box 4295
    Utica, NY 13504-4295
    www.vocalny.org

Notes

[1] Conna Craig, "What I Need is a Mom: The Welfare State Denies Homes to Thousands of Foster Children," *Policy Review,* The Heritage Foundation, Summer 1995, Number 73.

[2] Ibid.

[3] Richard Wexler, *Understanding Child Abuse Numbers,* Issue Paper 6.

[4] Richard Wexler, *Wounded Innocents: The Real Victims of War Against Child Abuse* (Buffalo, New York: Prometheus Books, 1990), p. 236.

[5] Geraldine Sealey, "More Rilyas?" ABCNEWS.com, June 5, 2002.

[6] Brian Ross, "The Lost Children," ABCNEWS.com, May 16, 2002.

[7] Conna Craig, op. cit.

[8] Kate Hilpern, "Made to Love," *Guardian Unlimited,* Guardian Newspapers Limited, July 11, 2001.

[9] Gurwitt, Rob. *"Raising a Neighborhood: Hope Meadows."* Innovations 3 Fall 2001.

[10] Richard Wexler *"Foster Care vs. Family Preservation: The Track Record on Safety,"* Issue Paper 1.

[11] "Threats to Children: A Generation Under Siege." Family Research Council 1992:103.

If you are interested in contacting Chandra Moyer to speak or minister in your community, please call:
Fruit of the Spirit Ministries

....

Phone (757) 546-2545
Fruitspirit@juno.com

Printed in the United States
60812LVS00002B/184-234